The Script Alphabet

BY ARTHUR BAKER

ART DIRECTION BOOK COMPANY, NEW YORK

Library of Congress Catalog Card Number:
78-56103
ISBN: 0-910158-43-6 (cloth)
 0-910158-47-9 (paper)

Published by
Art Direction Book Company
19 West 44th Street
New York, N.Y. 10036
Printed in the United States of America

The true form of the script letter
is a product of centuries of breeding - as
truly a thoroughbred in the world
of the graphic arts as its distinguished
ancestor, the Roman letter.

Tommy Thompson

4

6

8

9

Aabc
defghiyklmn
opqrst
uvwxyz

12

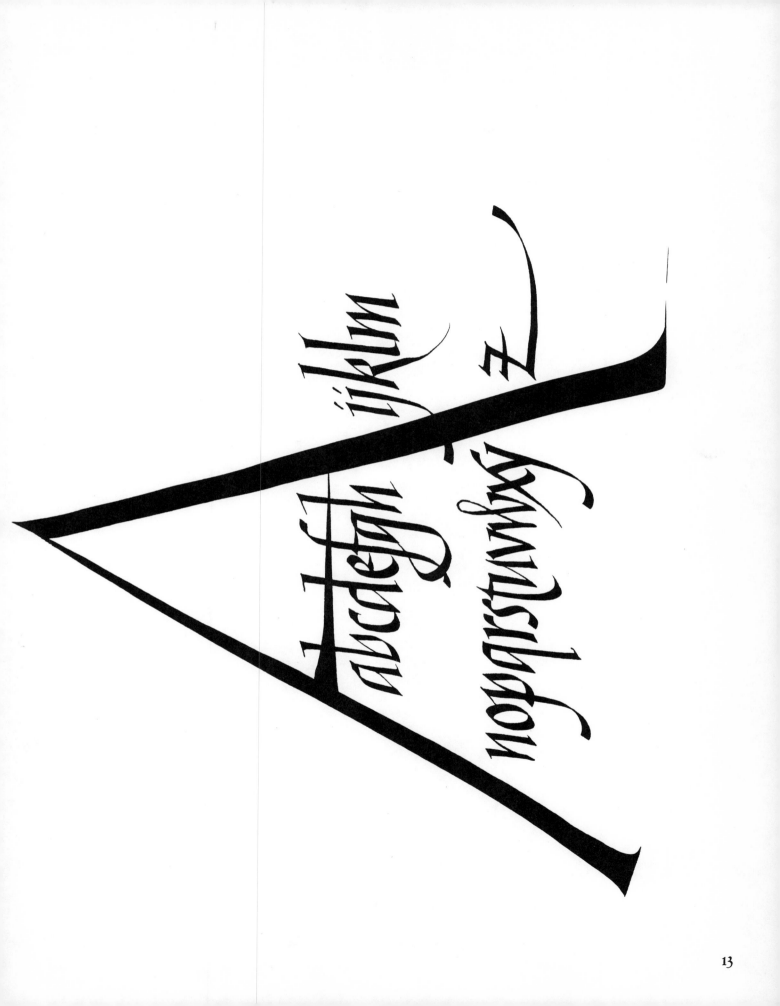

16

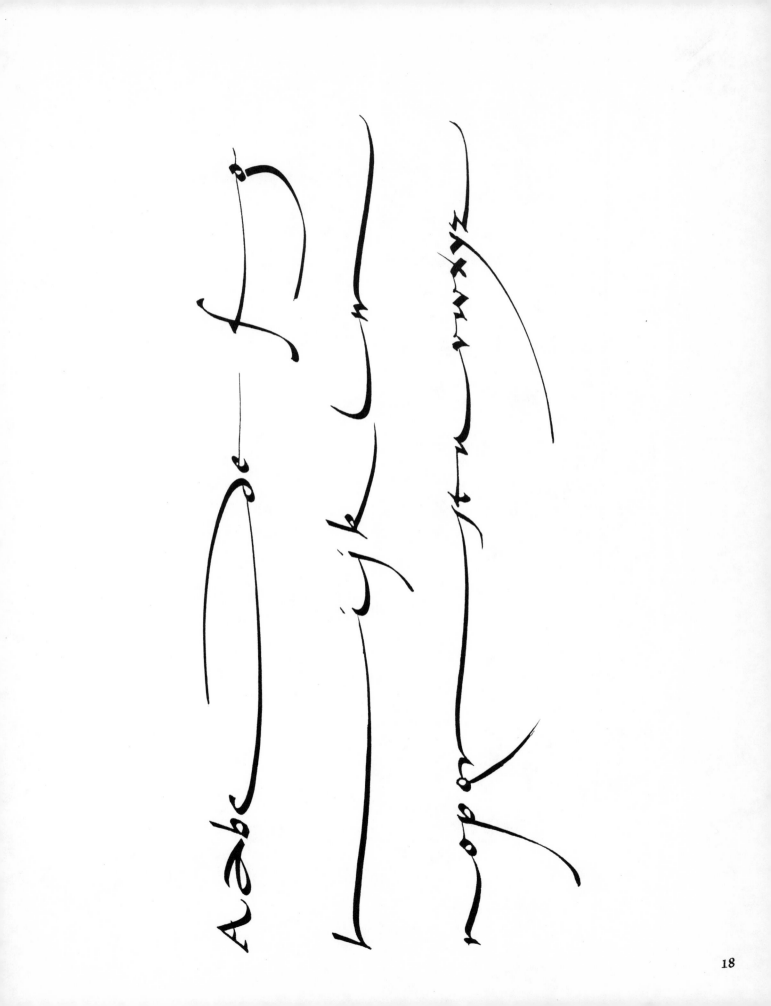

20

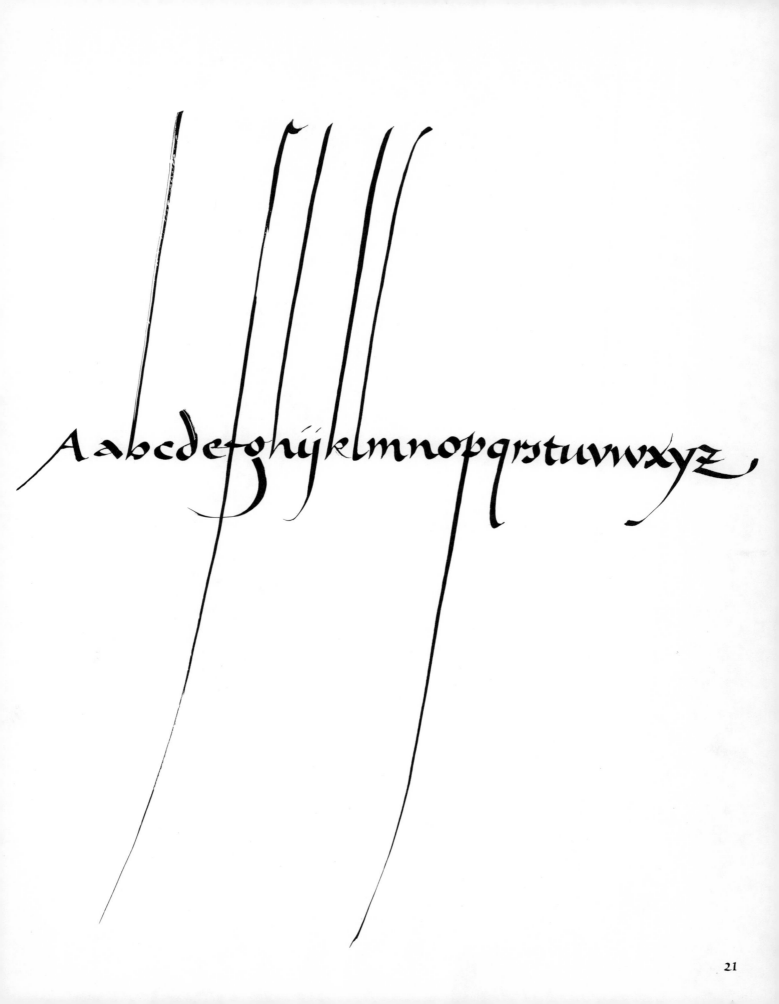

Aabcdefghijklmnopqrstuvwxyz

22

Aabcdefghijk
lmnopqrtuvw
xyz

abcdefghijkl
mnopqrstuvwxyz

34

Aabcdefghiijklmnopqrstuvw
xyz

41

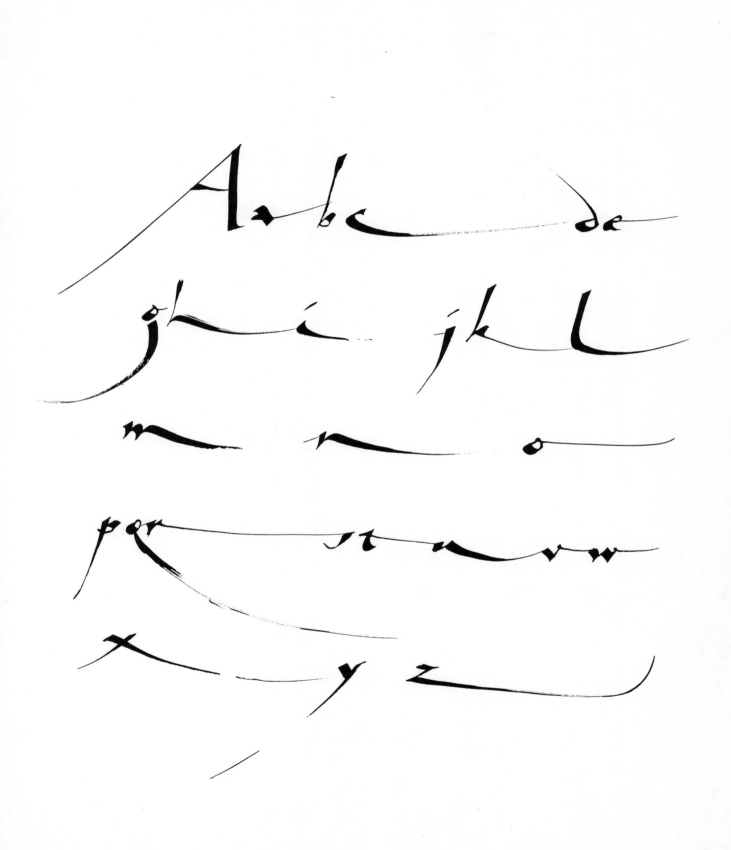

abcdefghijklmnopqrstuvwxyz

44

Aabcdefg
hijklmno
pqrstuvw
xyz

45

50

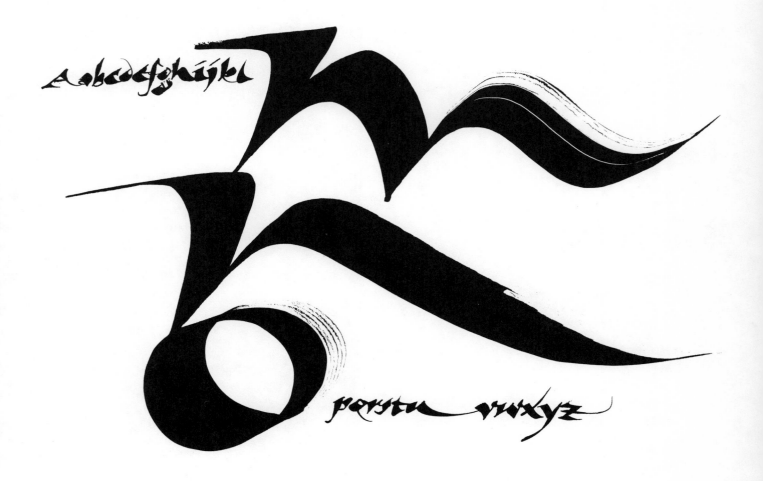

Aabcdefghijkl

pqrstu vwxyz

51

55

Aabcdefghijklm

nopqrstuvwxyz

60